C000186650

# THE LITTLE BOOK OF
# E-TYPE
# JAGUAR

Written by Charlie Morgan and Stan Fowler

# THE LITTLE BOOK OF
# E-TYPE
# JAGUAR

This edition first published in the UK in 2008
By Green Umbrella Publishing

© Green Umbrella Publishing 2009

**www.gupublishing.co.uk**

Publishers Jules Gammond and Vanessa Gardner

Printed and bound in China

ISBN: 978-1-906635-52-7

# Contents

# Introduction

AN INNOVATIVE SPORTS CAR OF the first degree, the E-type Jaguar captured the imagination of car enthusiasts the world over with its sleek, stunning looks, its exhilarating performance and its sensible price when it took to the road in 1961. It was an instant sensation and a winner for Jaguar for 14 years. In a *Daily Telegraph* article in March 2008, the E-type was voted in at the top spot (with four times as many votes as any other car), in a survey to find the 100 most beautiful cars of all time. Interestingly, more modern cars were convincingly overlooked and it was the classic cars that won through overall. The E-type caused a stir when it was launched more than 40 years ago and with the recent survey findings, perhaps it's no surprise that this stylish British sports car still has the ability to turn heads today.

Manufactured by Jaguar between 1961 and 1975, the E-type had a competitive edge second to none. First, it was priced well below other sports cars of its time, which enabled Jaguar to sell in excess of 70,000 vehicles in their 14-year reign with the E-type, and second, it was a fast car (for its day) with optimum performance. Designed as a two-seater coupé, as both a fixed head coupé (FHC) and as a convertible or open two-seater (OTS) the E-type was intended for long distance driving. Described by Enzo Ferrari as "The most beautiful car ever made", it was undoubtedly *the* car to be seen in during the 1960s and early to mid-1970s.

Four basic models were produced, but for many fans of the E-type, it is the original 3.8 litre car (built between 1961 and 1968) which holds most appeal. The original Series 1, as it became

RIGHT A row of five D-type Jaguars, the team which won the Le Mans Grand Prix five years running

known, had charisma and style, despite its flaws and with its long nose, hunched rear and fared-in headlights, became one of the most instantly recognisable icons of the 1960s. Next came the Series 2 quickly followed by the Series 3, while Jaguar also developed the Lightweight E-type (possibly a follow-up to their earlier D-type) and a one-off experiment, in the guise of the Low Drag Coupé.

When the E-type was launched in March 1961, the first 500 cars off the production line had flat floors and external hood latches. Today, these cars are relatively rare and more valuable. Under the bonnet, the engine comprised a 3,781cc version of the XK six-cylinder engine. The car was distinctly modelled on the Jaguar D-type which had been designed (as had its predecessor the C-type) as a racing car. The factory-built D-type with its upgraded 3.8 litre engine, was innovative during its four-year history between 1954 and 1957. With its single (or monocoque) chassis, it was tailored to aircraft engineering standards, rather than comprising an internal framework covered with a non-load-bearing skin. The idea in car manufacture was revolutionary

(although monocoque construction had been used in aircraft since the early 1930s) and gave the racing car aerodynamic efficiency. The driver's "tub" was made of aluminium alloy which was attached to more aluminium which formed a sub-frame carrying the bonnet, front suspension, steering assembly and engine. The rear suspension and rear drive were subsequently attached to the single chassis while the fuel was carried in "bags" inside the cells of the chassis; a further aircraft innovation. Following a career with Bristol Aeroplane Company during the Second World War, the legendary Malcolm Sayer joined Jaguar and was largely responsible for the aerodynamics of the D-type. In an effort to engage optimum speed and reliability, the long nose was added to the D-type for the 1955 racing season. Mechanically, the car shared many features with the C-type, including the groundbreaking disc brakes and the XK engine, but larger valves and an asymmetrical cylinder head were all new. When Jaguar withdrew from the racing world, unfinished D-types were roughly adapted for more practical use. Becoming a Jaguar XKSS, the car was given an extra seat and a second door as

LEFT A Jaguar D-type racing past Goodwood House

well as a full-width windshield and a folding top which was somewhat primitive. It was this dynamic car that was to set the scene for the iconic E-type that was to follow.

As with previous Jaguars, it was expected that the company's next car would follow in the same vein as those based on the imagination and vision of Sir William Lyons, but with the D-type having been cleverly mastered by Sayer, the E-type was undoubtedly his too. The mechanics were sophisticated with a unique structure courtesy of chief engineer William Heynes. But, despite being the ultimate in class, style and obviously an upwardly mobile sports car, the E-type gained its roots from a much earlier proto-type. Lyons' father ran a piano sales business in the early 1920s. It was here that the Swallow Sidecar Company (SS) was formed in 1922. William Lyons, together with his friend William Walmsley, who lived on the same street in Blackpool, designed and developed a motorcycle under the Swallow name. At the time, Walmsley was effectively working out of his garage, building sidecars which he then bolted onto reconditioned old military motorcycles. With big ideas and deter-

mination from William Lyons an overdraft of £1,000 helped with expanding the business and eventually they employed a small team for the production of their sidecars. In 1926, SS became the Swallow Sidecar and

Coachbuilding Company and Lyons and Walmsley began fashioning an existing car with more modern appeal. The Austin 7 (popular and inexpensive) was chosen for the initial project and SS created the 1927 Austin 7 Swallow Saloon. "Sidecar" was then dropped from the company name. Lyons was a determined businessman and the company left its birthplace in Blackpool to establish itself in Coventry at the heart of the motoring industry. Rather than

being a flight of fancy, the move was instrumental to the growing success of the company.

The factory in Blackpool had only been capable of producing two Austin Swallows a day. When Lyons received an order for 500 cars from Henlys it was essential to move the business to larger and more efficient premises. He quickly found an old Shell filling plant on Whitmore Park in Coventry (although it was later renamed Swallow Road) and SS moved to its new location at the end of 1928. As well as establishing a production line of 50 cars per day, the company also worked on other coachwork projects on established models such as Fiat, Wolseley and Swift which were first shown at the 1929 London Motor Show. Although coachbuilding had served Lyons well, he was keen for more challenges and set about becoming a car manufacturer in his own right. In a bold move, at the time of the Great Depression in 1931, he launched his first car, the SS1 coupé at the London Motor Show along with the smaller (1 litre engine) SSII. The car was relatively inexpensive at £310, although its impressive style, some would argue, warranted a higher price. But Lyons was

shrewd and realised that by fashioning the vehicles himself, for which he had an incredible talent, and keeping production runs prolonged, it enabled the company to keep prices down and affordable. It was this combination of slick lines and realistic pricing that was to make Sir William Lyons infamous.

The SS1 coupé, however, did not deliver all that it promised. Regrettably, the mechanics did not live up to the outside of the striking car with its choice of 2 litre or 2.5 litre six-cylinder Standard side valve engines. Lyons had struck a deal with Standard over the engines and by 1933 the new improved SS1 coupé with its new chassis was born. The car was still intended as a would-be sports car and the company again changed its name to SS Cars Ltd Motor Company. The year was 1934 and Lyons' ambitions did not match with those of his co-founder. It was at this time that Walmsley decided to leave the company. It was not until 1935 that the "real" sports car arrived in the guise of the SS90, so named for the speed it could achieve. The new two-seater open-top, as with all of Lyons' preferred designs, sported long smooth wings. It was to become a trademark style for

LEFT The Austin Swallow made by the Swallow Sidecar Company which eventually became Jaguar

RIGHT The Standard
Motor Company stand
at the 1935 Motor
Show

which SS would find itself famous. While the SS1 coupé had been capable of speeds of around 75 mph (120 kph) the SS90 could push the speed that bit higher reaching 90 mph (144 kph). Designed much to the same specification as the SS1, the SS90 had a shortened chassis and a Standard side valve engine together with a competitive price tag of £395. However, disappointment reigned when only 23 cars were sold. The problem factor had proved to be the engine. Lyons' turnaround in fortune was delivered by his meeting Harry Weslake, a tuning specialist. Weslake began working on the limited Standard engine but what the company really needed was sound engineering. This arrived in the form of William Heynes, who was appointed as chief engineer; in fact, at the time, he was the only engineer in the department.

While 1935 saw Weslake converting the Standard engine under the bonnet of the SS90, Heynes had just six months to prepare a new range of saloons ready for the London Motor Show. By now, connotations about the company name, "SS" were not conducive to successful business, given the events already underway in Hitler's SS in Germany so by the time Heynes, who had miraculously met his deadline, was ready to show off the new range at the show, the name had been changed to SS Cars (Jaguar), still known as SS Cars. Bird, animal and fish species had been put forward for the new company name under the direction of publicity manager, Bill Rankin. Jaguar was the instant winner.

Sidecar manufacture eventually became known as Swallow Coachbuilding Co (1935) Ltd based in Birmingham. The Helliwell Group bought out the company in 1945 where they continued to produce sidecars at their Walsall Airport works under a patented trademark. This side of Helliwell's business was closed down in the late 1950s. However, with unparalleled success, Lyons went from strength to strength. Even at the outbreak of the Second World War, aged just 38, the former junior salesman had already produced 5,378 cars and was running a public company. But he had not achieved this formidable and impressive company on his own and his understanding of who would work best, ensuring his ambitions could reach fruition, had brought together Heynes,

Rankin and Weslake alongside purchasing manager Arthur Whittaker and innovative engineer Walter Hassan. It was this winning formula that would make the Jaguar name synonymous with the British sports car. However, when the Second World War loomed, for the time being, there was other work

to be done.

The company turned its attentions to repairing Whitley aircraft fuselages, under manufacture, during war-torn hostilities. SS Cars also worked on the Stirling and the Meteor (the UK's first operational jet). But, Lyons was not completely unaware of his own ambi-

tions at this time and was also busy preparing for the post-war era, which, was scheduled to be "anytime soon". The company now had the talented Claude Baily who was instrumental to engine design development as the lack-lustre Standard engines had clearly reached retirement age. Lyons was desperate for a 100 mph (160 kph) saloon and lengthy discussions took place about how to achieve this seemingly impossible dream. A power unit was to be produced without the need for special tuning, so with the thought that 160 bhp was essential, the challenge was on and everything developed at this time was marked "X" for experiment. First came the XF (1,360cc), followed by the XG (1,996cc) and the XJ (also 1,996cc). With moderations from Harry Weslake, the XK was born but apart from Lagonda Rapier sports cars (produced 1934-1939) no British manufacturer had ever built a twin-cam before. Lyons was adamant that the engine needed to look as good on the inside as it performed on the outside and he was substantially happy with the XK. Under Weslake's guidance, the stroke had been increased from 98 to 106 mm (the bore remained at 83 mm) and a capacity of 3,448cc was reached. The cylinder head, made of aluminium, was standardised and the crankshaft ran in seven main bearings. It was undoubtedly this engine that would become the company's post-war fortune.

Not only was it substantial enough to power the required saloon, it was to become an essential ingredient of the E-type that was destined to take the world by storm.

# Jaguar Cars Inc, USA

WHEN THE E-TYPE WAS LAUNCHED in 1961 its readiness was timed to coincide with the Geneva Motor Show in March and the New York Show in April that year. Jaguar couldn't possibly have imagined the storm that the car would cause at either event and the Americans couldn't get enough of the new car. Such was the popularity of the model that more than 72,500 cars were sold during its 14 years of production, although 75 per cent of these were manufactured for the left-hand drive market which demonstrates Jaguar's global appeal.

Jaguar would have struggled to maintain their dominance in the market and indeed the demand for their latest coup, if it wasn't for Jaguar Cars Inc, their US distributors who were set up and managed under the watchful eye of Johannes "Joe" Erdmans, who was responsible for the company's transatlantic sales. Erdmans, from Holland, arrived in the US in 1952 and was particularly successful at engineering Jaguar's move into exports. Two other men were also

**LEFT** Jaguar interior

ABOVE Jaguar XK120

instrumental to the company's success across the Atlantic; Max Hoffman, who was responsible for sales in the east of the United States and Chuck Hornburg, who operated on the other side of the vast country. In 1954, under the direc-tion of Erdmans and Hoffman, Jaguar Cars North American Corporation was established on Park Avenue, New York. The company eventually became known as Jaguar Cars Inc, US and was ready to show off the E-type on 1 April 1961.

# Before And Alongside The E-Type

FOLLOWING THE SECOND WORLD War, Jaguar was looking for something new. Despite the fact that Sir William Lyons did not feel as strongly about his sports cars as he did his saloons, the company produced the XK120 which was only their second ever sports model. The car was fitted with the innovative XK six-cylinder engine and the XK120 was modelled around the engine rather than the other way around. In short, the XK120 was designed in order for Jaguar to show off its new engine in time for the London Motor Show in 1948. The saloon model, the Mark VII, which had been intended as the car to launch the new engine was overlooked in favour of the sporty number. However, the XK120 had to be prepared in record time to meet the October date in the capital. It was designed to be a limited edition with either a 2 litre engine or a 3.4 six-cylinder engine. But, the launch of the car at the motor show

ABOVE 1953, Jaguar XK120 FHC coupé

would bring its own surprises. In fact, such was the popularity of the car that Jaguar could not meet the demand and just under 200 models were built on the old-style methods of alloy body and wooden frame. Frantically, Jaguar tried to prepare itself for full-scale production with steel bodywork.

Jaguar now found itself with success both on and off the racetrack and the C-

type, developed specifically for racing under the expert supervision of Malcolm Sayer, was soon underway. The C-type eventually made way for the D-type which was followed, of course, by the legendary E-type. However, the XK120, XK140 and XK150 had all made their mark and between 1948 and 1961 Jaguar had sold just short of 30,000 models.

The XK120 which dominated the market between 1948 and 1954 was designed as an open two-seater roadster as well as a fixed head coupé and a drop-head coupé. The XK140 also had three models with these variants, although the XK150 had just two variants as already discussed (the fixed head coupé and the open two-seater coupé). However, the XK150 wasn't actually originally designed as a two-seater roadster; this particular variant took to the roads in 1958.

The Mark VII was the company's entirely new saloon and, like the XK120, was one of the first cars to be fitted with the new XK six-cylinder engine. Although it didn't make the London Motor Show in October 1948, the car was none the less the epitome of luxury and excitement for the consumer. Its refined style and optimum performance made it an instant success when it eventually appeared at the motor show in 1950. As with all Jaguars, the car was extremely competitively priced and would go on to become one of the company's "best sellers" of all time. Although by sports car standards the Mark VII was huge, it proved a worthy car in both circuit racing and rallying and as with other Jaguars proved its worth when it became a success in the United States. The car was eventually upgraded to the Mark VIIM and in 1957, when the car received further development its name was subsequently changed to the Mark VIII. The following year it was again renamed, this time to the Mark IX. This car would remain in production until the same year that the E-type would make its debut.

The Mark X was a complete re-design of the original Mark VII and its upgraded variants. The car went on to sell more than 46,000 models and became the leading Jaguar car of the decade. From 1955 to 1969, Jaguar also concentrated on their "compact" saloons which had been brought about through expansion in increased sales and growing success in the face of competition. The compact saloons were, like the E-type, built around a monocoque chassis while a front sub-frame was fitted separately to carry the suspension, steering and hefty weight of the XK engine. The bodywork was designed to be tough and strong although the overall structure was a great deal lighter than previous saloons.

The XK engine helped to provide the

LEFT Jaguar XK150 sports car

**RIGHT** A sleek Jaguar
XK150, 1960

compact saloons with top speeds that beat off the competition although the engine capacity was only 2.4 litres. It was a success from the moment it was launched and later the engine capacity was increased to 3.4 litres. The compact saloon would remain a success for the company until 1959 when three new models were introduced. The Mark 2 came in a 2.4 litre, a 3.4 litre or 3.8 litre engine and was a significant improvement on its predecessor in terms of its handling ability. Like the compact saloons, the Mark 2s were an instant success and more than 90,000 were sold before 1967. The popularity of the car was, quite simply, phenomenal. Coming off the production line alongside the Mark 2s was the Daimler 2.5 litre V8 following the company's purchase of Daimler in 1960. The Daimler was first introduced two years later and was to become the most popular of all the company's models at that time. Daimler had never known anything like it. As the saloons produced over two decades had proved to be Jaguar's most prolific and highly sort after models, it was little wonder that Sir William Lyons had a strong affection for them.

# Chapter 2

# The Team
# And Location

## Sir William
## Lyons (1901-1985)

FOR 50 YEARS, SIR WILLIAM LYONS was the man behind Jaguar. The quintessential Englishman, Lyons was born on 4 September 1901 in Blackpool. His early days were filled with a keen interest in motorcycles; he owned a Sunbeam but dreamed of Harley Davidsons and Brough Superiors. When he eventually owned a Norton motorcycle he bought a Swallow sidecar from William Walmsley whereupon he was able to show his phenomenal business sense. He persuaded his older neighbour (Walmsley was 10 years his senior) that he could expand his business by using a few of his own ideas. For motoring enthusiasts, this would prove the catalyst for conceiving and developing one of the most exciting car manufacturers of the 20th Century. But it wasn't just Lyons' business acumen that brought the fledgling company success, his unique sense of styling was quite clearly ahead of its time and even early in his career, he was beginning to distinguish the characteristics in his designs that would embody the Jaguar trademark with sharper, more sleek, lower profiles.

Deciding not to follow his father into the musical business, Lyons left Arnold

**ABOVE** Heynes had a major impact in the engine design of the Jaguar XK120 lightweight

School and began an engineering apprenticeship with Crossley Motors in Manchester. At the same time he was studying at the technical school. Then, in 1919, Lyons headed back to Blackpool where he became a junior salesman for Brown and Mallalieu, the

Sunbeam dealership. By the early to mid-1960s, Lyons had become the highest paid British executive with a six-figure salary. By this time he had already become Sir William, having been knighted in 1956 for his services to British industry and the success he had made of exporting his cars to an international market. In 1966, faced with an ever-increasing strength in what was a global industry Jaguar was merged with the British Motor Corporation (BMC) to form British Motor Holdings; later absorbed into British Leyland. Having kept an extremely tight reign on his company, even following the merger with BMC, Lyons retired in 1972 to take up a life of rearing prize-winning sheep and cattle on his farm in the village of Wappenbury in Warwickshire.

Lyons married Greta Brown in 1924 and the couple had three children, John (born 1930), Patricia (1927) and Mary (1937). Sadly, at the young age of 25, John Lyons was killed in a road accident in 1955 on his way to the Le Mans 24-hour race. Although he received no formal training, Sir William Lyons was an extremely talented man, who largely made his designs through three-dimensional mock-ups rather than through drawings. He was behind the design of almost all Jaguar cars except the C-type, D-type, E-type and XJ-S. Some have argued over the years that the reason Lyons was somewhat less than enthusiastic about the E-type was because he hadn't actually designed it himself.

Others take the view that the great man of style was more interested in the saloon cars (indeed the XJ6 was his favourite) that Jaguar built. For Lyons, it seems, the sports cars that his company produced were second in line in terms of volume and ultimately profitability. He died at his home, Wappenbury Hall, on 8 February 1985. Lady Greta died the following year. The prestigious accolade, The Guild of Motoring Writers' Sir William Lyons award is presented to a young motoring journalist each year by Jaguar Cars Ltd.

# William Heynes
(1903-1989)

BORN IN LEAMINGTON SPA, WARwickshire, on 31 December 1904, the infamous motoring engineer William Munger Heynes was undoubtedly the most influential person behind Jaguar after Sir William Lyons. He attended Warwick Public School where his aptitude for sciences meant that his science master tried in vain to encourage the young Heynes into a life of surgery. As one of six boys, however, the resources needed to medically train Heynes were

**RIGHT** The Jaguar C-type was a racing car that won Le Mans a number of times

way beyond his family's resources. Instead, he went to work for Humber, in Coventry, as an apprentice in 1923, but two years later found himself as part of the design team. He remained with the company for a further 10 years where he took up the reigns as head of the technical department within five years of joining the team. He moved to SS Cars as Lyons' chief engineer in 1935 where he discovered that he had six months to prepare the company's next range of cars for that year's London Motor Show. He proved both his worth and his abilities when he managed just that.

Heynes found the young Lyons (only two years his senior) serious and determined with the ability to say exactly what was on his mind. It didn't seem to bother Heynes though as he stayed with the company until his retirement in 1969. He worked long hours and as hard as his boss but was asked if he was ill when, after two years without a break, he asked if he could have a holiday. He obviously had an undisputed respect for Lyons who made his engineer director of engineering and vice chairman in 1961. He had previously become a director in 1946. Although by Coventry standards SS Cars and ultimately Jaguar

**RIGHT & BELOW**
Sayer used sliderules and log tables for his complicated car design calculations

were small compared to the likes of the huge motor industries such as Daimler, Humber, Hillman, Rover, Triumph and Riley, Heynes managed (with just one apprentice initially) to build an engineering department which earned the respect of the motoring capital. Alongside Claude Baily, Walter Hassan and Harry Weslake, Heynes was significant in the development of the XK engine. His C-type won Le Mans in 1951 on its debut and was instrumental in ensuring the racing reputation for which Jaguar is still synonymous today.

# Malcolm Sayer
## (1916-1970)

ONE OF THE GREAT PLAYERS OF Jaguar was designer and aerodynamicist Malcolm Sayer. Instrumental in the

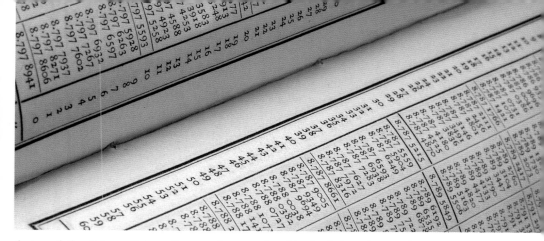

design of the C-type, D-type, E-type and XJS, Sayer was born in Cromer, Norfolk in 1916 and became one of the first engineers to apply aerodynamic principles to the design of cars. He was accredited by Sir William Lyons as being one of the most influential men in the Jaguar story. Educated at Great Yarmouth Grammar School, where his father was a teacher, Sayer then moved to what was formerly Loughborough College. When the Second World War broke out, Sayer was exempted from conscription by "reserved occupation protection" as he worked for the Bristol Aeroplane Company in the aero engine department. In 1947 he designed the bodywork for the Gordano sports car before he joined Jaguar in 1950 and

became pivotal in the design of some of the company's most successful post-war cars. Having gained extensive experience with Bristol Aeroplanes, Sayer was used to a working environment of wind tunnels and smoke testing in aerodynamics. He brought these skills to Jaguar. However, prior to joining one of the most dynamic motoring companies, Sayer and his wife moved to Iraq in 1948 following the birth of their first daughter where he was to take up a post at Baghdad University. The job never quite materialised and Sayer instead worked on government vehicles before his return to the UK two years later. Sayer and his wife, Pat Morgan, had a son and another daughter born in 1953 and 1956 respectively. Sadly, the charm-

ing, unassuming Sayer was struck by heart disease and died at the age of 54 in 1970. He is still remembered as one of the great innovators of introducing the slide rule and seven figure log tables used to work out formulae that he invented for drawing curves. Today, this work is carried out by complex computer software programmes.

# Frank "Lofty" Wilton England
(1911-1995)

BORN IN FINCHLEY, NORTH LONdon on 24 August 1911, Frank Raymond Wilton England, often referred to as "Lofty", was the man responsible for managing Jaguar racing during the 1950s. Eventually, when the company retired from racing, Lofty England was to take up the positions of chairman and chief executive, succeeding Sir William Lyons, when he moved into mainstream management.

England developed an interest in motoring from an early age and was apprenticed as an engineer to the Daimler Motor Company in 1927 where due to his tall stature (he was 6' 5") he quickly earned his nickname. Having watched Bentleys being road tested along the A5 when his family moved to Edgware, he had predominantly been interested in working for them, but his application to join the company was unsuccessful. So, it was to Daimler that he went and it was here, during his five-year apprenticeship, that he began a career in motor racing; he finished second in the inaugural RAC Rally. As an enthusiast, England became mechanic to Sir Henry Birkin and Whitney Straight and in 1938 he moved to Coventry as a service engineer with Alvis. He joined the RAF where he served in the Royal Air Corps as a Lancaster Bomber pilot on daylight bombing raids.

He returned to his former company after the war and established a long friendship with Walter Hassan. Through Hassan, England joined Jaguar as a service manager in the mid-1940s. In 1956, he became service director and during Jaguar's heyday on the racing circuit he also took up the coveted role of racing manager. By the early 1960s, Lofty England was promoted to assistant managing director and deputy-

LEFT Frank "Lofty" England chatting with the racing driver Mike Hawthorn

**ABOVE** Harry Weslake provided the engines for the winning Jaguars at Le Mans in the 1950s

managing director in 1966. In 1967 he went on to become the company's joint managing director. He took up the reigns of chairman and chief executive in 1972 although he was aware that the roles would be short-lived; he was already 60 at the time. What was a difficult decision during his time at the helm, however, was the decision to halt production of the E-type in 1974. It was the same year that England would retire. He died in May 1995 in Austria.

# Harry Weslake
## (1897-1978)

BORN IN 1897, HARRY WESLAKE designed his first carburettor when he was just 17 years old. This led him to a prolific career with the likes of Norton, Vanwall, BRM, Coventry Climax, Chrysler, AAR Eagle, Ford and, of course, Jaguar designing cylinder heads. While at Jaguar, the cylinder head specialist began work on modifying the side valve Standard engine. He also went on to develop the overhead valve version of the Morris series A engine (used in the Morris 1000) and the Mini. Weslake was also the founder of Weslake Engineering which he set up in Rye, East Sussex.

As well as being a high profile engineer, Weslake was also passionate about shooting and fishing. He died while watching his own Weslake powered bikes at the old Wembley Stadium in London. He was in his eighties. The former industrial site where Weslake Engineering was established lay derelict for some time until it was bought and refurbished and renamed Weslake Industrial Park.

# Walter Hassan
## (1905-1996)

THE OUTSTANDING ENGINEER Walter (Wally) Hassan was said to have

**ABOVE** A 5.3 V12 engine in a 1992 XJS

been encouraged to work in the motoring industry by his uncle who was a model shipbuilder. He first studied at the Northern Polytechnic before enrolling at the then Hackney Technical Institute of Engineering. Born in London on 25 April 1905, Hassan found his first job with Bentley Motors working under the supervision of Frank Clement in the experimental department. As a creator, Hassan left the company when it was taken over by Rolls-Royce and began building his cur-

riculum vitae with a job for Wolf Barnato. In 1933, he began constructing a racing car (known as the Barnato Hassan) which proved its high speeds. He then went on to develop a car for Bill Pacey called the Pacey Hassan during the racing heyday of the 1930s.

In 1938, Hassan moved to SS Cars where he played a pivotal role in the formation of the XK engine and the V12 engine during two of his three stints with the company. As chief development engineer at SS Cars, he garnered a distinguished career before leaving for Coventry Climax. Here he was responsible for 30 different types of engine including the V8 (a winning success) before he returned for the final time to Jaguar as group chief engineer. He worked past retirement age until 1972 (he was 67) and received the OBE for his services to motor sports. Hassan died in July 1996.

# Harry Mundy
## (1914-1988)

HARRY MUNDY WOULD HAVE A distinguished and varied career. Born in Coventry in 1914, Mundy left school to begin an apprenticeship with Alvis in 1930. Then he travelled to Lincolnshire to work at ERA in Bourne where he took the role of draughtsman. Here, he met Walter Hassan who was to become his life-long friend and collaborator on the inspired V12 Jaguar engine. He stayed for three years until 1939 then returned to Coventry as a senior designer for Morris Engines.

When the Second World War broke out in September that year, Mundy was an acting wing commander and engineering officer in the RAF but went on to join BRM in 1946 as head of the design office. Four years later he joined Coventry Climax as chief designer following the problems at BRM with the V16 Formula 1 engine. It was Hassan who persuaded him to join the company. The FWA engine of 1954 which Mundy designed with Hassan was one of their great successes. Highly competitive, the engine went on to dominate the racing scene of the mid-1950s. However, Mundy then decided on a change of career and left Coventry Climax in 1955 to become the first technical editor of *The Autocar*. Despite his new job, Mundy still worked on the design of the twin-cam engine for Lotus.

Having worked for the magazine for nine years, in 1964, Mundy was persuaded, yet again by Hassan, to change his job. This time he would join Jaguar and the two friends once again collaborated on one of the most revolutionary and exciting engines; the V12. The engine went into production in 1972 and Munday remained with the company until his retirement in 1980. Even in retirement he found time for some consultancy work. Mundy died in 1988; he was 75 years old.

# Derrick White
## (1929-1970)

**ABOVE** White was responsible for the Lightweight E-type

BORN IN LONDON IN 1929, DER-rick White was a talented chassis engineer who was instrumental in the development of lightweight E-types. His love of all things motor racing had come from his family roots. His father, Robert "Bob" White, took his family from east London to South Africa where he was involved in organising the first South African Grand Prix. When he graduated from university, Derrick White became a pilot but was deeply committed to building cars and he arrived in the UK in 1952 as an experimental draughtsman. He first joined Connaught, but the company's misfortunes saw White return to his new homeland in South Africa.

He returned to the UK in 1959 where he joined Jaguar and the innovative early days of the E-type. As his real love was for motor racing, White couldn't help but bring those elements to the new Jaguar range. This led to the Lightweight E-type and the Low Drag Coupé. However, some of White's ideas for the cars were vetoed by Heynes and in 1964 he moved to Cooper as chief engineer. After the demise of his new company, White subsequently moved to Surtees Honda in 1967 and then to Triumph based in Coventry in 1969. His time at the company would be short-lived, however, when White died of a brain disease the following year. Tragically, he was just 41 years old.

BELOW The historic Brown Lane's Jaguar car plant before its closure

# Browns Lane
## (Coventry)

WHEN JAGUAR MOVED ITS PRO-
duction facilities to Coventry in 1952 it
was a small "fish" in a very large "pond".
As the heart of the motor industry, the
city was home to many of the leading
car manufacturers of the time. Jaguar
would more than prove itself a match
for its contemporaries and would establish itself as one of the most enduring
manufacturers of all time. Running the
entire length of the Browns Lane site,
including production, corporate offices
and eventually the Jaguar Daimler
Heritage Trust, the historic home of
Jaguar remained here for more than 50
years; it eventually closed in 2005.

The entire site, which was originally
government-built for the production of
Bristol aero engines at the threat of the
Second World War, was constructed in
the mid to late 1930s. Just under 253,000
square metres of land (about one tenth of
a mile) was proposed as an additional site
at Allesley to the north west of Coventry.
Originally, the land had been home to
Daimler where it was responsible for
building Bristol aero engines throughout

the war. But, not long after hostilities
ended, Daimler had little use for the land
known as Shadow 2. It was then that
Jaguar stepped in, desperate for more
space. The company went on to buy
Daimler in 1960 and the original land

ABOVE The Jaguar factory in 1956

(Shadow 1) also became Jaguar's. Production at Browns Lane was set to wane as Castle Bromwich in Birmingham became the preferred location alongside Halewood Body & Assembly for assembling Jaguar cars. All but the head office, museum and wood veneering facilities had moved from Browns Lane by 2005 when the site was closed. It was bought by Macquarie Goodman in 2007. All Jaguar facilities were then located at the Whitley plant, also in Coventry.

# Chapter 3

# Series 1: 1961–1968

THE E-TYPE ROADSTER AND FIXED head coupé were unveiled at the Geneva Motor Show in March 1961 to universal acclaim in a world premiere. Two E-types were sent to Geneva with one example being presented to journalists in the Eaux Vives Park, while the other was the sensation of the year on the stand at the Geneva Show. It was also well received when it made its bow at the New York Motor Show the following month and America soon fell in love with the marque. Its futuristic styling and outstanding technical attributes convinced not only the motoring journalists, but also made a deep impression on the public.

The cars featured a monocoque – French for "single" (mono) and "shell" (coque) – body with a front sub-frame, two seats and a rear luggage door on the coupé. The first automotive application of the monocoque technique was Lancia's 1923 Lambda and a few years later in 1934, both Chrysler and Citroën built the first mass-produced mono-coque vehicles with the innovative Chrysler Airflow and the Traction Avant respectively. So while the monocoque technology was not a totally new inno-vation, improvements in the manufac-turing process now allowed separate parts to be combined into single stamp-ings that reduced weight and assembly costs, as well as increasing structural rigidity and improving door fitment.

Costing £2,097 for the roadster and £2,196 for the coupé (a revelation when Aston Martin's rival DB4 retailed at £3,968), the E-types were initially sold with a three-carburettor version of the 3,781cc six-cylinder XK engine that produced 265 bhp at 5,500 rpm and was meshed to a four-speed Moss gearbox.

Although the engine was already 13 years old, it was defined by many as the most advanced production engine in the world and having powered the XK series since 1948, it would continue to be installed in Jaguars until 1986. The original 3,442cc engine had been developed during the Second World War specifically to drive a new luxury saloon (that would emerge in 1950 as the Mark VII) at speeds of 100 mph.

Featuring a double overhead camshaft, a cast-iron block and a seven-bearing crank with an aluminium cylinder head, it also boasted separate timing chains (top and bottom) and the two

RIGHT Headturning
wire wheels

valves per cylinder optimised performance giving 160 bhp at 5,000 rpm.
Refinements carried out during the
1950s increased the capacity of the
engine bringing the power to 220 bhp
from the enlarged 3,781cc that drove
the Mark IX saloon and XK150 and cul-
minated in the power plant that was
unveiled in the first E-types that were
able to do 0-60 in 6.9 seconds.

Other modifications included the fitting of a manual choke and a separate
header tank between the radiator and
the engine that reduced the necessary
height and allowed for the design of the
sleek body that has been admired for
almost 50 years. Obviously there were
other measures that individual owners
could take to increase the engine's
power such as replacing the SU carbs
with Webers although the North
American federal exhaust emission reg-
ulations meant that cars headed for
that continent from 1968 were supplied
with two Zenith-Stromberg carburettors which, combined with a revised
manifold, produced less residue at
low speeds.

Early problems, however, included
drastic oil consumption (sometimes as
much as 200-300 miles per pint) and a

tendency to overheat but many enthusiasts still yearn for one of the first cars off
the production line. It wasn't until a second fan was installed on the Series 2
cars in 1968 that the latter problem was
overcome. But, such was the reliability
of the engine that it was claimed owners
could expect it to last for up to 200,000
miles if properly looked after.

A bigger bore offered a larger 4,236cc
engine in 1964 but the arrangement of
four of the six cylinders had to be
moved slightly in order to keep the
overall block size the same. Other modifications included straightening the
inlet manifold tracts, installing a Lucas
alternator instead of the original
dynamo and a pre-engaged starter
motor - all of which gave the larger
engine the same power output as the 3.8
litre version but with increased torque
(up from 260lb/ft to 283lb/ft at 4,000
rpm). It also discouraged prolonged
cruising over 5,000 rpm which could
on occasion result in crankshaft
damage and a hefty repair bill. The
on the road price for these cars was
£1,896 for the roadster while the coupé
retailed at £1,992.

The gearbox had also been around for
some time, in this case since 1946 and

would be utilised in every manual Jaguar until 1964. With the same ratios as had been used on the XK150S, the four-speed box was married to a 10" Borg and Beck single plate clutch but it became synonymous with a crashing first gear and changing between the other gears was only made easier by mastering the art of double declutching. This problem was alleviated by the introduction of a new all-synchromesh gearbox that coincided with the arrival of the 4.2 litre engine in 1964. Now lubricated, inertia baulk rings ensured

the 2-plus-2 that was unleashed in March 1966. This conventional box offered three selections – L (Lock-up), D1 and D2. With the central T handle positioned in D1, the car automatically changed through all the gears but if you selected D2 only second and top were available which provided a smoother ride and greater fuel economy. The new model was 9" longer than the coupé and boasted a revised rear bulkhead that allowed the addition of a rear seat.

The front suspension had been taken from the design that had worked so well over the years with the D-type, with forged wishbones being used top and bottom along with a torsion bar and telescopic dampers. But it was the set-up at the rear of the car that raised a few eyebrows.

Independent suspension had been tried on various cars built in Europe but without much success. Jaguar, however, had mastered the problems where others had failed and the layout designed under the supervision of William Heynes caused great interest when unveiled. Rather than having the body mounted on leaf springs that keep each opposing wheel perpendicular to the other, Heynes' team created a steel sub-

that the gears could not be engaged until they were synchronised which, together with a Laycock diaphragm clutch, provided a smoother ride.

Customers were first given the option of an automatic gearbox (at an extra cost of £140) with the introduction of frame that housed the entire suspension as well as the differential, hub carriers and disc brakes. With this assembly connected to the body by just four rubber mountings (plus two radius arms and their respective mountings), this innovative design allowed each wheel to independently rise and fall vertically along the surface of the road thereby improving the handling and safety of the car while providing a smoother ride for its passengers. While this was of great comfort while driving, it was a hindrance to maintenance and even the simplest of tasks often involved dropping the whole unit out of the back end of the car.

The E-type was steered via a rack and pinion system that was popular at the time. With the rack running across the car behind the radiator joining the two front wheels, the driver's instructions were transmitted from the steering wheel via a universally-jointed steering column. With the ability to turn the steering wheel two and a half rotations to change from one lock to the other, it gave the E-type a turning circle of around 35 feet - not bad when you consider today's XF at 16' 3" long (compared to the E-type at 14' 7") has a turning circle of 37 feet.

One of the few areas to come under frequent criticism was the brakes but Jaguar, always alert to negative comments and the publicity that accompanied them, were constantly redeveloping their set-up in an attempt to provide a braking system that adequately matched the performance needs of the E-type. January 1962 saw the introduction of modified master cylinders while a revised pedal and power leaver followed four months later. Just over a year later, thicker rear discs and better callipers further alleviated the stopping problems although the braking system that accompanied the arrival of the 4.2 car was altogether better and provided fewer heart-stopping moments.

The E-types were supplied with wire wheels, something that has gone out of fashion today with the technological advances in their alloy counterparts but it is a throwback to a more romantic era of motoring that many find aesthetically pleasing. Originally fitted with Dunlop RS 6.40x15 crossplies, by late 1965 it was Dunlop's SP41 radials that the car would be wearing - although it was possible to order racing tyres for a

car to enhance performance. The advantage of the radial tyre was that its construction allowed for the sidewalls and crown of the tyre to have separate functions which gave greater traction and a longer lifespan.

As previously mentioned, it is easy to see that the E-type's distinctive looks were largely inherited from the D-type. Malcolm Sayer was credited with the end result although Sir William Lyons was also responsible for artistic input. The front end of the car was a framework of tubing that was designed to take the stresses of carrying the engine and front suspension. This was anchored to the monocoque shell that ran backwards from the front bulkhead, encompassing in the passenger compartment and the rear of the car. The curved panels were constructed by Abbey Panels while Pressed Steel Fisher built the inner sections with the whole lot being put together at Browns Lane.

As with many roadsters, it was the two hollow sills along each side of this section (between the wheel arches) that provided the greatest strength of the construction. The structure was further strengthened by the steel floorwells (that were revised at the end of 1961 as taller customers complained about the

lack of leg room), the transmission housing and propshaft tunnel as well as a transverse member running under the seats. Box members were welded to the floor of the boot and the inner wheel arches with others added to the rear bulkhead (which was also modified to allow for the seat to be adjusted) to take the strain of the rear suspension radius arms. Obviously, the roof of the coupé provided added strength and the roadster later came with an option to buy a glassfibre hard-top (at a cost of £76) that could conveniently be fitted with the mohair hood in place. As a soft-top, the roadster was reasonably comfortable and waterproof with the hood up, however, it was prone to excessive wind noise despite the fact that each hood was tailored to the individual car in Jaguar's own trim shop.

The bonnet was constructed in three sections (centre and wings with the joints concealed by chromium plated moulding) and was designed to be hinged at the front end of the car, thereby allowing easy access to the engine compartment as required. The bonnet might seem heavy to lift, but that action was aided by counterbalanced springs and the external Budget

locks were replaced with internal versions in September 1961 to cure vibration issues. The "muscle car look" was further enhanced by the power bulge and accompanying louvres (that also helped with cooling the engine) as well as the distinctive front lights. These may have looked attractive but the toughened glass covers dispersed the light beams and failed to provide adequate lighting when driving at night in adverse weather conditions - a problem rectified with the introduction of the 4.2 model that boasted more powerful sealed beam headlamps. At the other end of the car was the luggage area, very restricted on the roadster – although there was an area behind the seats where smaller items could be stowed.

The rear lights differed on the roadster and the coupé due to obvious restrictions of the body while the car was finished off with decorative chrome trim and a bar that bisected the oval air intake. A trio of two-speed wipers were installed to keep the large wrap-around windscreen clear and this only added to the individuality of the E-type.

The interior of the cockpit was just as eye-catching as the car itself, with a central aluminium panel housing many of

LEFT Series 1 E-type Jaguar from the front

the instruments as well as leaving space for a radio and twin speakers. White figures on black faces adorned the Smiths oil pressure, water temperature, fuel and ammeter gauges while the matching speedometer (calibrated to 160 mph) and rev counter that incorporated a clock were traditionally positioned in front of the driver. There was a separate key ignition switch and a starter button.

The aluminium finish was repeated on the handbrake shroud while the Coventry Timber Bending Company produced the steering wheel which was finished in wood with three aluminium spokes. Connolly hide adorned the bucket seats above a plush carpet (again, these seats would be improved in the 4.2 along with many other interior modifications) with seat-belt anchoring points standard since January 1962. The coupé saw the introduction of an optional heated rear screen in April 1962.

Jaguar, noting that families wanted to be seen in their flagship vehicle and having to keep up with competitors who had already introduced rear seats for children in their sports cars, introduced a 2-plus-2 in March 1966 that was 9" longer than the standard coupé and incorporated a small bench seat in the rear. To accomplish this, Jaguar had increased the size of the cockpit – in height as well as length that gave the car a more upright appearance – and the doors were now more than 8" wider. There was more room for luggage, a parcel shelf and a bigger transmission tunnel that could accommodate an automatic gearbox while the springs and dampers were uprated to deal with the extra weight.

Jaguar made minor refinements to the E-type Series 1 at the end of the following year – including exposing the headlights to improve visibility – and these cars have affectionately become known as the Series 1 ½ as they bore many of the modifications that were featured in the fully revamped Series 2 that Jaguar unveiled in October 1968. The previous eared hub-caps were replaced by circular ones and a mirror was added to the driver's door.

Inside the cockpit there were more modifications including a revamped facia with rocker switches being replaced and a hazard warning light being added. The heater controls were also revised along with the demisting vents to provide better operation. One

main feature of this car was the new doors which had had to be redesigned to incorporate "burst proof" locks as dictated by American legislation.

The Series 1 had outdone Jaguar's initial expectations and it had taken time to get production up to a level that could come anywhere near coping with the demand. More than 2,000 cars were sold by the end of 1961 (and hasty production measures had to be put in place to cope), a figure that was double the company's original estimate for total sales. Indeed, it had initially been envisaged that they might only sell 250 E-types, although this was quickly revised and overtaken. By the end of 1963, 12,491 cars had been built making it the best-selling Jaguar sports car ever - a figure that smashed the previous record of 12,055 held by the XK120 which had taken five years! 1966 was also to prove a record year with 6,880 cars being built - the most popular being the 2-plus-2 at 2,627.

**ABOVE** The E-type's sleek lines have made it a classic

# Chapter 4

# Low Drag Coupé: 1962

RIGHT E-type Low
Drag Coupé in action
BELOW View of the
Low Drag engine

FOR JAGUAR TO BE FALLING BEHIND its rivals on the racetrack was unpalatable and so the Low Drag Coupé was developed as a successor to the all-conquering D-type. It was conceived by

Derrick White and Tom Jones in early 1962 and was based on the production E-type, using the steel monocoque but with other body panels – such as the bonnet, doors and boot lid – constructed from lightweight aluminium. Previous Jaguar racers were built as open-top cars because they were based on ladder frame designs with independent chassis and bodies. So conscious were they about bringing the overall weight of the car down to a minimum that even the glass windows were replaced with Perspex alternatives (with the exception of the windscreen).

The rear end of the car was redesigned by Malcolm Sayer to give better aerodynamic performance and was aesthetically pleasing to the eye - even with the rear door welded shut. Rear brake cooling ducts were installed next to the rear windows and the inte-

**ABOVE & RIGHT**
E-type Low Drag Coupé

rior trim was discarded, with insulation only around the transmission tunnel. In all, these modifications gave the Low Drag Coupé a top speed of an impressive 170 mph.

A tuned version of Jaguar's 3.8 litre engine was used but, unfortunately, air management became a major problem and – although much sexier looking and certainly faster than a production E-type – the car was never that competitive. It seemed the faster it went, the more it wanted to do what its design dictated; take off. But it has since been recognised as a crucial turning point in the development of the Lightweight E-type that followed.

The original plan was for several of these lightweight cars to be built and raced but the eventuality was that just one example was produced. This specimen was owned by the factory until 1963 when it was sold to Dick Protheroe, a Jaguar racing driver who enjoyed success in both England and Europe with his car bearing the registration "CUT 7". Since then it has passed through the hands of several collectors on both sides of the Atlantic and now is believed to reside in the private collection of the current Viscount Cowdray.

Several replicas have been built by companies such as Tempero Cars and Vicarage although they are reasonably expensive. At the start of the 21st Century, Temperos were offering their Low Drag Coupé (built completely from aluminium) for around £68,000 - a snip when you find out that a Lightweight E-type in need of total restoration sold for almost £440,000 the same year!

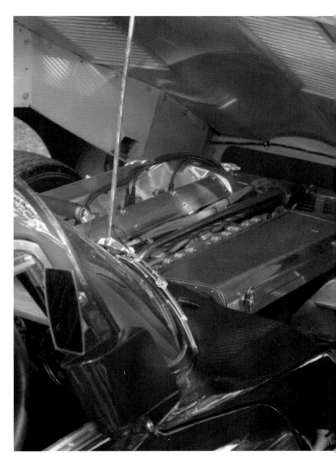

# Chapter 5

# Lightweight E-Type: 1963–1964

IN SOME WAYS, THE LIGHTWEIGHT E-type was understandably an evolution of the Low Drag Coupé to replace the outdated D-type that had proved so successful. With at least one exception, it remained an open-top car in the spirit of the D-type to which this car is a more direct successor than the production E-type which is more of a GT than a sports car. Ferrari had just won the 1962 GT Championship so Jaguar wanted to design a new competitive racing car. They were made available to Jaguar distributors or private teams with a proven track record and entered into various races but, unfortunately, unlike the C-type and D-type racing cars, they did not win at Le Mans or Sebring where they were unable to outpace the Ferrari GTOs although they were more than a match for competitors such as the Corvette and Cobra.

Originally dubbed the Special GT E-type, the Lightweight E-type made extensive use of aluminium alloy in the body panels and other components although the production steel engine frames were kept. They were powered by a 300 bhp-plus alloy block 3.8 litre Lucas-injected XK engine with dry sump lubrication and many other modifications, such as a boot lid ventilation slot to help get rid of heat from the rear inboard brakes.

Although they performed well at circuits such as Silverstone, Goodwood and

Nurburgring, their development had reached a peak by the mid-1960s and from then on were only seen at club events. Jaguar planned to produce 18 units but ultimately only a dozen lightweight cars were built between March 1963 and January 1964. As such a rarity, the history of these 12 cars has been well documented. They are sought after by collectors and have been known to change hands for seven-figure sums.

One of the cars was destroyed by fire while being driven by Roy Salvadori at Le Mans in 1963. The Briton – partnering American Paul Richards – was an experienced Formula One driver who had participated in 50 Grands Prix between 1952 and 1962 but only managed 40 laps of the 31st Grand Prix of Endurance before disaster struck. Since then it has been rumoured that two others have been converted to coupé form but the Lightweight E-type has been acknowledged as a significant milestone in Jaguar's history. Again, Tempero Cars offer a replica that is built more solidly than the original which had a tendency to crack under stress. That's acceptable for a racing car that was only supposed to last one race, but not really suitable for an investment that will set you back £88,000 plus a donor vehicle.

LEFT Lightweight Jaguar E-type

# Chapter 6

# Series 2: 1968–1971

WHEN THE SERIES 2 WAS OFFicially unveiled at the 1968 London Motor Show, many of the obvious modifications that had shown up earlier on the Series 1 ½ were more apparent. Yes, the headlights were bigger and now external (as opposed to being covered) and thereby reduced the car's top speed by a couple of miles per hour but the air intake had been enlarged by 68 per cent which improved the airflow. This was due in part to compensate for the overheating problems that had dogged the Series 1 but it was also dictated by the new air conditioning system that was to be offered as an optional extra on cars exported to the US. Other optional extras included power steering and chromium-plated disc wheels instead of the traditional wire counterparts. One other modification that alleviated

the overheating was the replacing of the single engine-driven fan with a twin electric-fan unit to cool the new crossflow radiator.

One of the main differences between the two models was that Jaguar dispensed with the 3.8 version and only offered the Series 2 with the larger 4.2 engine. The cars retailed at £2,163 for the roadster, £2,273 for the coupé and £2,668 for the 2-plus-2 making any of the three models a reasonably priced alternative to many of Jaguar's competitors of the era.

The braking system received its first major overhaul in seven years as the original Lockheed units were ditched in favour of Girling brakes with three cylinder callipers. This increased the area of the discs used for braking and provided increased stopping power.

Externally, the original thin

bumpers were replaced with larger wrap-around ones and the decorative intake bar became thicker. The rear lights were also enlarged and mounted beneath, rather than above the bumper while twin reversing lights were introduced. The exhaust tail pipes now protruded from either side of the car due to the number plate being lowered.

Structurally, little had changed from the Series 1. The rake of the front windscreen on the 2-plus-2 was increased from 46 ½ degrees to 53 ½ degrees, thereby moving the bottom of the screen towards the front of the car to make it appear less upright. This did, however, mean that there was not enough room for the three-wiper set-up and the car reverted to the more traditional pair of wipers.

In the cockpit, right-hand drive cars benefited from the US-style interior that saw a new dashboard installed. The final month of 1968 saw the fitting of a steering column lock while the following May saw the introduction of perforated leather trim and modified head restraints. Jaguar continued to tinker with numerous areas of the car including redesigned

camshafts in November 1969, a revised clutch operating rod in March 1970 and a revised handbrake lever on the 2-plus-2 two months later.

The first full year of production, 1969, saw a record 9,948 cars built at Browns Lane. This total comprised 4,287 roadsters, 2,397 coupés and 3,264 2-plus-2s but numbers dive-bombed over the next two years with only 3,781 being delivered in 1971. It was time for a change and Jaguar responded with the Series 3.

# Chapter 7

# Series 3: 1971–1975

MUCH HAS BEEN WRITTEN IN THE intervening years about the disappointment felt by many E-type enthusiasts when the Series 3 was introduced in March 1971. True, the car did have a larger and more powerful 5.3 litre V12 engine but it was widely argued that the car into which it was installed was outdated and outclassed. Ironically though, the 14,983 V12s that were built have today become one of the most sought-after versions of the E-type.

The launch took place at Palm Beach and was attended by Sir William Lyons on what was his farewell trip to the US. At the age of 69, he was retiring the following year. He was accompanied by Harry Mundy, one of the brains behind the V12 engine that Jaguar hoped would keep them competitive in America. Jaguar initially offered the Series 3 with an option of the 4.2 XK engine or the new V12 but soon withdrew the former as demand for the 5.3 grew.

The 5.3 was the only V12 of the era that was manufactured in significant numbers; both Ferrari and Lamborghini had their own versions of the V12 but these were produced in relatively small quantities. In order to cope with the new power plants, Jaguar spent £3 million upgrading its Radford factory so that it could cope with the manufacture of these larger units.

As with the original 3.8 engine, the 5.3 was not specifically designed for the E-type. It had begun its life during the 1950s with racing in mind, although it was temporarily shelved once Jaguar pulled out of competing in 1956 and did not enjoy a test run until August 1964. It had been envisaged to run the engine in the 1965 Le

Mans race but Jaguar did not have a suitable car.

Work began on a mid-engined racer, similar in set-up to the Formula One cars of the time and work began on the XJ13. The new prototype was not entered at the following year's Le Mans and – when Jaguar merged with the British Motor Corporation – testing suggested that it wasn't as fast as anticipated. The company was particularly worried about news of the project being leaked to the press as rumours of a V12 E-type would have dramatically hit sales of the six-cylinder model and Jaguar simply weren't ready to put the new engine into production. It was a case of back to the drawing board.

So it was that 1971 saw the revamped V12 engine being "roadtested" in the Series 3 in preparation for its installation in the new XJ12 that arrived the following year. Jaguar used the E-type as a guinea pig so that any teething problems could be ironed out before the launch of its flagship saloon. The original intention had been to use a fuel injection system being developed by Brico but it was decided to stick with the traditional carburettor set-up and each set of three cylinders was fed by a

Zenith-Stromberg 175CDSE carb.

The Series 3 was only offered as a roadster and a 2-plus-2 coupé, both sharing the latter's longer wheelbase. This meant that the roadster gained extra luggage space as well as more room for seat adjustment. Obvious modifications included flared wheel arches and a bigger front air intake that housed a grill that was likened to a bird cage. An air scoop was also added underneath the intake to increase ventilation throughout the car. This was supplemented by an extractor grille on the luggage door of the 2-plus-2 and the rear pillars of roadsters that were fitted with hard-tops.

Changes to the suspension saw the use of longer wishbones from the Mark X/420G and driveshafts which increased the rear track of the Series 3 which now came with 6" steel wheels as standard rather than the wired predecessors. As the car was heavier than the Series 2, the braking system was overhauled as well, with ventilated Girling discs installed on the front and power steering was now standard. The rack and pinion was modified in December 1972 following a report of a car not heading in the direction dictated by the driver.

Roadster customers were given the option of going with the traditional four-speed manual or they could upgrade to the automatic gearbox that had been available on the 2-plus-2 for the previous five years. Until March 1973 the exhaust system ended in a four-pipe fantail but this, like the rest of the car, was prone to rust and was replaced by a twin outlet with a modified silencer.

Inside the cockpit, Jaguar attempted to modernise the E-type with a smaller, leather-trimmed steering wheel, perforated leather seats and a fresh air ventilation system. The 2-plus-2 saw the front seats raised to provide better visibility while also giving the rear passengers more foot room and it was now possible for those in the back to recline the seat in front of them to make exiting the car easier.

Prices had increased with the roadster retailing at a cost of £3,123 and the 2-plus-2 for £3,369 – still drastically less than their competitors – but Jaguar found that cars were sitting longer on the forecourts of dealerships and new customers were no longer having to join a waiting list. American legislation was also dictating modifications to the fuel

tank and that a roll bar must be added to the 2-plus-2. Other, global, factors were also thrown into the mix such as the Arab-Israeli war that had broken out in October 1973 causing oil prices to spiral out of control leading to a decrease in demand for fuel-thirsty cars.

It was therefore decided to cease pro-

duction, with the final E-type being manufactured in September 1974; the decision was made public five months later. In a marketing ploy that backfired, Jaguar shipped all bar one of the final 50 roadsters in black, fitted them with wire wheels and installed a plaque in the dashboard of each that was signed by Sir William Lyons. (The penultimate car was painted in British Racing Green.) Sadly, these didn't fly out of the door as quickly as had been intended and several were sold at a reduced price. One of the reasons that these cars took so long to sell was that the public were reportedly keenly awaiting the arrival of the E-type's replacement, widely anticipated to be another sports car. As it turned out, the next Jaguar was the XJ-S which, at £8,900 (more than double the price of an E-type), was the most expensive vehicle the company had ever retailed.

Today, these V12 E-types are cherished as much for their refined ride as their look and suit those more interested in a luxury sports car rather than a rugged muscle car that provides a more lean driving experience. In 1975, however, it was the end of a golden era for British motoring as well as Jaguar themselves.

LEFT A line of new Jaguar E-type cars under dust sheets at Coventry, 1972

# Chapter 8

# After The E-Type:
## XJ-S And The XK8

RIGHT The Jaguar
XJ-SC

JAGUAR HAD TO HAVE SOMETHING that was going to stun and wow in the same way that the E-type had done and its answer was the XJ-S. Many of the Jaguar faithful thought the company would replace the ever-popular sports car with another, but circumstances intervened and Jaguar sports cars came abruptly to a halt. For some time car manufacturers had been abandoning the idea of roadsters and open two-seaters. It seemed that the consumer wanted something bigger added to which legislation was requiring cars to become more and more safety conscious. This was particularly prevalent thinking in the US and Jaguar had little choice but to follow suit if it was to maintain its position in the top echelons of the manufacturing world. The need and demand for more refinement, more comfort and greater versatility in an everyday car had arrived. The heyday of the E-type was well and truly over.

The XJ-S (later becoming the XJS) was a luxury tourer of the type required by an ever-demanding market and the first model made an appearance in 1975 (as a 1976 model). It was powered by the V12 engine and came in either manual or automatic, although the manual's shelf-life was short-lived. Rivalling the sports cars of Lamborghini and Ferrari, the XJ-S could accelerate from 0-60 mph in just 6.5 seconds and had a top speed of 157 mph. However, the car pre-

miered in the wake of the fuel crisis when markets were relatively small. The car also faced a fair amount of criticism that it was an unworthy successor to the E-type. Valiantly, Jaguar persevered and ignored the comments about the "flying buttresses" behind the windscreen. For ardent Jaguar enthusiasts the car was just as prolific as the E-type it had come to replace and it proved just as worthy on the racing scene.

By 1983, Jaguar introduced a new

cabriolet version of the XJ-S, called the XJ-SC. However, the rear seats were abandoned and Jaguar, once again, had themselves a two-seater vehicle. It was not a full convertible and this came in the guise of the Hess & Eisenhardt XJ-S which originated in the US market. The official Jaguar full convertible did not hit the roads until two years later in 1988 while other variations of the model appeared up to 1991.

At the beginning of the 1990s the XJ-S underwent a complete revamp and overhaul and was renamed the XJS. The rear windows were larger and there was a new 4 litre version while the V12 was increased to 6 litres in the mid-1990s. Also, when the re-engineered car was launched a convertible was in the offing although the "flying buttresses" were kept as Jaguar appealed to the market audience that they were part of the car's character and charm. Even the rear brakes had been revamped and were now fitted with outboard rear discs as opposed to the complicated inboard brakes that had appeared on all previous models. It was just the change that the XJS needed and in 1994, further improvements were made with more aerodynamics around the front of the vehicle and to the rear. In addition a 2-plus-2 convertible was introduced – catering for a wider audience – and the car was exported to the US that same year. Further revisions came in 1995 to the 4 litre AJ6 engine. The XK8 succeeded the XJS when it ceased production in 1996 after 21 years.

Like all Jaguars the XK8 is sleek, innovative and highly desirable. It came to fruition to replace the aging XJS as a grand tourer. Making its debut at the Geneva Motor Show in March 1996, the XK8 was to become available as a coupé and a convertible. It was the first Jaguar car to encompass an eight-cylinder engine with the AJ-V8. The XK8 was also offered with either a supercharged 370 hp engine or a 290 hp engine; the supercharged engine is known as the XKR. Like the Aston

**LEFT & BELOW** The Jaguar XJ-S

Martin DB7, the XK8 is derived from the Jaguar XJS. However, both the XK8 and the XKR are electronically limited to a speed of 155 mph which is 2 mph lower than the fastest speed of the XJS. Both types of XK8 have standard 18" alloy wheels although 19" and 20" wheels are available at extra cost.

As you would expect the XKR features are often standard (such as a navigation system and self-levelling headlamps) whereas these are optional extras for the purchaser of the XK8 model.

A limited XKR Silverstone was produced in celebration of the company's return to Formula 1 racing in 2001,

however only 600 models were built. With its platinum finish, high performance and improved transmission the car was destined for an exclusive market. Following the XK8, the XKR 100 was launched also in celebration in 2002; this time to celebrate the centenary year of Sir William Lyons while the XKR Portfolio convertibles were only ever produced for the US market in 2004. It was reputed that a universal Portfolio would be launched in 2008.

Further developments came with the XKR 4.2-S which was launched at the Geneva Motor Show in March 2005. This car was the last design to be based on the original model of 1996. In addition, Jaguar produced a concept car, the XKR-R which it was rumoured might be launched based on a Mk 2 XK (also in 2008). Whatever the likelihood of the new model may be, one thing that is clear is that Jaguar will continue to impress and please with some of the most beauti-ful cars to grace the world's roads. The smooth, sleek lines of the cars are recognisable the world over and what started out as a small operation in a garage in someone's back garden in the seaside resort of Blackpool has turned into one of the most successful and prolific car man-ufacturing stories of all time.

BELOW A Jaguar XKR on display at a 2005 motor show

# Chapter 9

# The E-Type Thoroughbred

JAGUAR HAVE LONG HAD A SUC-cessful tradition of producing competitive sports cars. The company was victorious at Le Mans in 1951 and 1953 with the C-Type, then in 1955, 1956 and 1957 with the D-Type (unbeknown to anybody, even Jaguar themselves, it would be another 31 years before a Jaguar took the chequered flag in this prestigious event). Sadly, although it certainly looked like a competition car, the E-type was most definitely a car designed for road use.

That's not to say that the marque didn't have its successes. Four weeks after the car's March 1961 introduction, former Formula 1 driver Graham Hill steered an E-type to victory in the British Automobile Racing Club's 25 lap GT race at Oulton Park. Further successes followed as the E-type began to make a name for itself on the racetrack. The E-types stood up well when unleashed on the tighter GT circuits and in shorter races but on the continent, however, they found themselves unable to keep pace with the V12 Ferraris.

The days of car manufacturers putting together an official works team were long gone but they were prepared to assist private owners and it was these people who kept the Jaguar name at the forefront of motorsport. People such as John Coombs, Peter Sargent and Dick Protheroe were entrusted with getting the best out of the cars and they were also instrumental in the

development of the Low Drag Coupé and the Lightweight E-type.

It was not just in Europe that the E-types were competing though. Mark Brennan won 39 out of 45 Sports Car Club of America races that he started between 1963 and 1965 while Bob Jane won the 1963 Australian GT Championship. The Jaguar E-type was very successful in US SCCA Production sports car racing with Group 44 and Bob Tullius taking the B-Production championship with a Series 3 V12 racer in 1975. Although never seriously challenging the domination of the Ferraris, the E-type enjoyed success both in Europe and the States from the early 1960s until it ceased production in the mid-1970s. The Americans even threw a "Tribute to Jaguar" event at Laguna Seca in California in 1976 which was in essence a farewell party for the E-type.

Since then, Jaguar have seen their cars compete in both the World Sports car Championship (WSC) Group C and the IMSA Camel GTP series between 1984 and 1993 with the XJR Sports cars, a series of race cars used by Jaguar-backed teams. It was one of these, an XJR-6 that

**LEFT** The Jaguar XJR-6 in action

RIGHT Jaguar D-type
on the race track

emerged victorious at Le Mans in 1988.

Jaguar used two different types of chassis for IMSA and WSC until 1988 when TWR were chosen to take over their team for both championships and built an identical car for both series, known as the XJR-9. The company withdrew from the WSC in 1991 to concentrate on the IMSA but withdrew from that event two years later. Jaguar did return to the

world of motor racing in 1999 when parent company Ford purchased Jackie Stewart's Formula 1 outfit. Sadly, results did not live up to expectations with just 49 points claimed from 85 Grands Prix and the team was sold to Red Bull in 2004. The motorsport fraternity eagerly awaits the next instalment in the illustrious history of Jaguar as a competitive racing car.

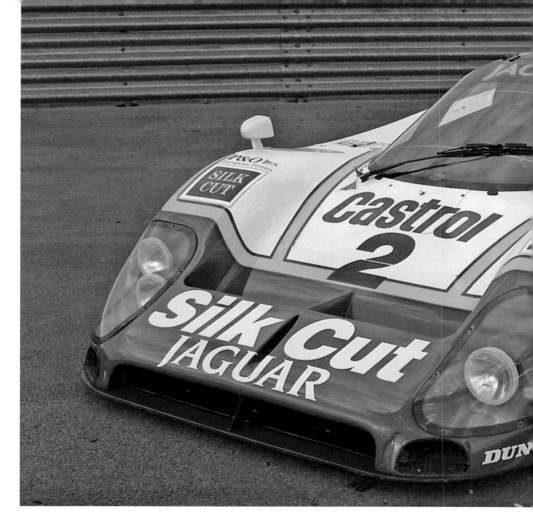

# Chapter 10

# Restoring A Jaguar E-Type

DAVE RAWLE, FROM BUDE IN Cornwall, was a man with a mission. He wanted an E-type as soon as he saw one in 1961, but it would be 40 years before he realised his ambition and owned the car of his dreams. Dave was adamant that he wanted a Series 1, but these cars are rare and he decided he couldn't be too choosy. Luckily, the car that he eventually found was a Series 1 3.8 litre left-hand drive manufactured in 1963 that hailed from Arizona but had at some point moved to California where it spent 13 years in storage before being shipped back to the UK.

Buying a secondhand E-type can be fraught with problems as they were extremely prone to rust. Believing that it

**LEFT & ABOVE**
The 1963 E-type prior
to restoration

is simply the sill that is rotten may prove to be a costly miscalculation once the repair work begins and further horrors are uncovered. While it is possible to pick up a roadworthy example for under £20,000, the majority of the cars available to purchase today can cost tens of thousands of pounds more. During the late 1980s and early 1990s, many investors sank their money into E-types as their value rose higher and higher but, in much the same way that house prices crashed, so the classic car values tumbled. Today, as the cars that are over 30 years old decrease in number, the E-type is back in favour by popular demand.

The Series 1 became Dave's in 2001, but it was four years before he had time to start his restoration project. With a strong desire to finish with an extremely drivable car, it was his intention from the outset to upgrade where necessary without detracting from the original look and style of the Series 1 and noth-

ing was changed that couldn't be put back while all original parts were retained. Although he had wanted to carry out all the work himself, for Dave, who had wanted to drive the E-type for more than four decades, time was of the essence and he decided to employ the services of a local restoration company

**ABOVE & RIGHT** The car required stripping down and disassembly

and a specialist engine shop. In July 2005, Dave's first priority was to strip the car down and photos of every stage were painstakingly taken in order to help with reassembly. Each part was logged on a spreadsheet to help the process. At first glance, the bonnet had plenty of filler around the air intake, otherwise, it didn't look too bad. There didn't seem to be any major accident damage although the engine waterways were heavily corroded.

The car looked "tired", perhaps unsurprising after 42 years and although most of the parts were usable,

LEFT & ABOVE The
body had to have all
paint and filler removed
before the car could
undergo a respray.

a large number needed replacing. Despite the problem with the waterways, the engine frames looked in fairly good condition apart from some jacking damage to the picture frame and radiator support. This involved several months of work on the smaller items while the paint and filler on the body panels were removed using a hot-air gun to minimise damage from excessive blasting. When the paint began to peel off in long strips, it became obvious that the car had undergone a respray on two occasions. The original colour was opalescent silver blue, but a darker blue had been used before the car was eventually sprayed white.

On the inside of the car, the job

**ABOVE & RIGHT**
Once all the paint was
removed the body was
treated with a zinc
primer

proved more difficult where sound-proofing had melted with time and a bad re-trim had made a real mess. Here Dave used the same method as he did on the outside of the E-type. Next, the electrical equipment was removed (it took a couple of days) and it was discovered that new looms were necessary. The originals were kept for comparison and wires were labelled where original colour coding was indistinct.

Once all paint and filler were removed with a plastic preparation wheel, the bare metal was treated with a coat of zinc primer. Moving to the interior, the foot wells had rotted completely and although the rest of the flooring wasn't too bad, there was some corrosion on the right-hand cross member and rust in the rear bulkhead (at floor level) was replaced. The inner and outer sills were in a reasonable condition, but eventually the outer ones were replaced. The driver's side bulkhead was badly distorted which was probably caused by jacking under the foot well. Dave points out that jacking in the wrong places had caused more damage to the car than would have been expected, even age allowing. The boot was in a complete mess and it was

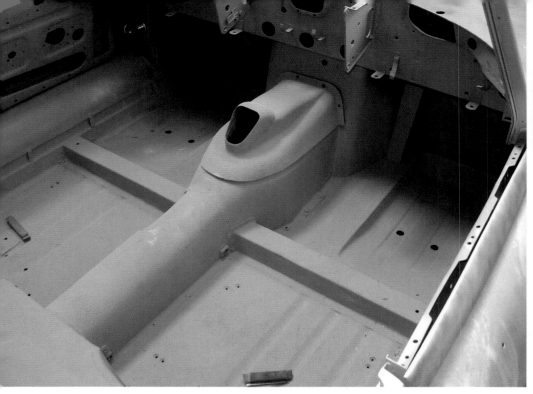

decided that blasters would be used. The distortion that Dave found in the centre box section was probably caused by a jack used to push out damage to the right-hand wing.

Added to this, once the fuel tank was removed there was evidence of damage to the wheel arches and the car appeared to have been hit at some point in both rear wings. The fuel tank was rusted through and had to be replaced but the good news was that the boot floor was in better condition than the interior floor. In particularly hard to reach places, POR15 Metal Ready was used to dissolve rust while

FAR LEFT & LEFT
The Guide coat inside
and out the E-type shell

more slide hammer holds in both
doors were MIG welded.

After six weeks of hard work, all but
the bonnet had been stripped from the
car and it was now ready for the restoration company.

However, that still left a lot for Dave
Rawle to do. His first job was to free the
seized door hinges as 17 years of stand-
ing had left the aluminium hinge seized
to the steel pin. After several days of
applying heat and penetrating oil, the
hinges were then blasted clean before
being primed. These were then sent to
the restorers who would check the gaps
before making a frame.

In September 2005, the Series 1 was
delivered to the restoration company
that specialises in Jaguars and
work swiftly got underway on the
purpose made jig, which the car fitted,
despite the previous accident damage,

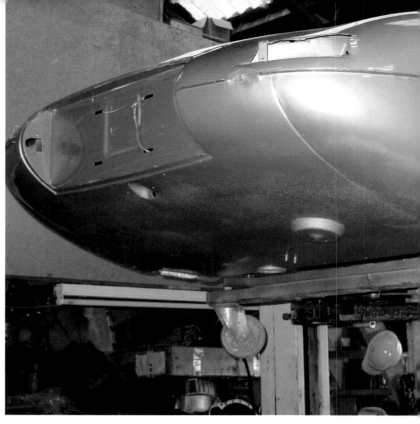

indicating that it was not out of line. The next job was to remove the IRS so that the brushes, bearing and seals could be replaced.

Before the floors could be removed safely, there were about 250 spot welds that needed to be drilled out. A special drill bit was used to drill through the old panel. The sill braces proved robust with only surface rust which meant that the whole area just required cleaning up and repainting.

LEFT The Jaguar regains its original blue coat

The replacement flooring was delivered with ready-made foot wells which saved some time replacing the rotten originals. However, Dave Rawle points out that nearly all replacement panels available for the E-type require some adjusting to fit and he advocates keeping as much of the original metal as possible. In the case of his Series 1, the new floors were too large by a few millimetres and had to be cut to fit the car.

The driver's side bulkhead was fixed

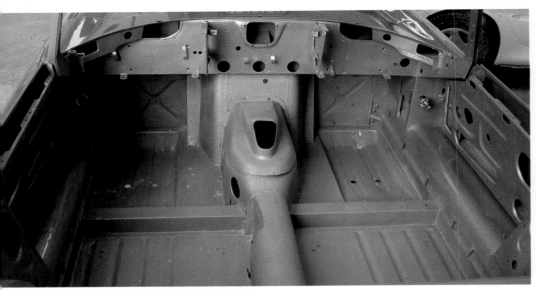

ABOVE Every part of the Jaguar's shell is coated in its original blue finish

RIGHT The finished body heads back for its rebuild

by a strip of new metal where it met the floor and although the floors were nearly finished at this point there was still a great deal of bodywork to do. The rear quarter panels revealed a combination of rust, accident damage and filler which made replacing them the best option.

Once the new floor was established, the interior instantly improved.

It was also decided to blast the inside

of the bonnet – like the boot and bulkhead – as using a heat gun would prove time consuming. However, to minimise the risk of damage, excess filler and paint were removed first. Next, the restoration company tackled the rear quarter panels where the right side proved more difficult as accident damage to the wheel arch needed to be fixed.

In November 2005, Dave Rawle received a call from the body shop

about the front right wing. Aside from accident damage it was full of ripples and filler while the top lip which joined to the centre section was almost eaten away. Dave decided to replace the wing as labour costs of fixing it would prove just as costly as buying a replacement. On the up side, plenty of panel beating around the air intake determined that the car was now taking on the characteristics of a Series 1.

The centre cross member (a square section), was modified to clear the output flange of the short five-speed Getrag gearbox while the original Moss box was replaced as one of several upgrades. As Dave had decided to use the E-type as a daily drive during the summer months, the underside was primed and sprayed with stonechip before being further sprayed with body colour for maximum protection. Next, the engine

**LEFT & ABOVE** The engine and suspension also underwent an extensive restoration

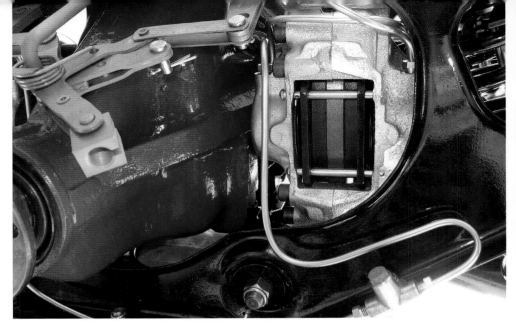

frames were removed so the bulkhead could be blasted. Before being reassembled, the bulkhead and frames were sprayed in the original colour of opalescent silver blue.

It took considerable work, but the replacement wing was eventually made to fit the rest of the bonnet.

Once the mudguards were re-bonded, the bonnet was sprayed with etch primer. Although the bonnet had, by now, been straightened, the next job was to set the height and gaps before taking the Series 1 to the spray shop where opalescent silver blue was applied. While waiting for the spray shop to carry out their work, Dave had time to catch up on the front suspension. Describing the job as akin to completing a jigsaw, he explains that the parts were either cadmium plated or just zinc plated as, later on in the production of the Series 1, cadmium became unpopular. He continues that: "Zinc has a low tolerance to acid and salt, an alternative is nickel, but that also has its problems and looks too bright to me". In order to get round the problem, Dave chose zinc/nickel alloy and clear passivate. With nickel comprising 14 per cent of the solution it is superior to zinc but looks just like cadmium plate.

Next the torsion bars were tackled and Dave found that after more than 40 years,

the essential tools were lots of penetrating oil and a very big hammer. Following this exercise, the paint job on the bodywork was finished. Dave was extremely pleased with the stunning result.

The next task was restoration of the independent rear suspension. Awkward and heavy, the IRS needed two people to

BELOW The cockpit electricals and dash start to be installed

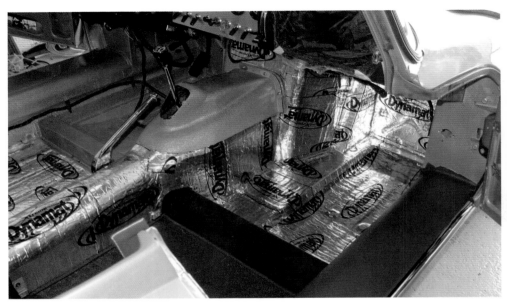

**ABOVE & RIGHT**
During and after the cockpit refurbishment showing the stunning transformation

move it, and Dave would advocate steam cleaning once it is accessible before stripping it down as this gives a clearer picture for reassembly.

Although the springs were cleaned and painted, it proved an arduous task and replacement costs are low. Dave discovered that the tag on the original differential had 46 crown wheel teeth to 13 pinion gear teeth (giving a US ratio of 3.54:1). This would have negated his need for fifth gear at motorway speeds so he compromised from the UK standard (3.07:1) with a 3.31:1 ratio giving a reduction of 13 per cent over the standard UK set-up. While the output shaft showed signs of wear, the bearing proved a surprise. Dave found a single, double race angular contact bearing (no longer available) rather than the Timkin roller

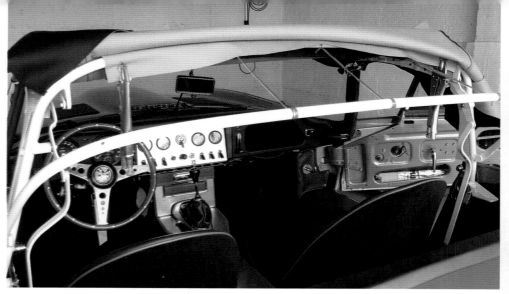

bearings he was expecting. The replacement kit included shims as the bearing is slightly narrower, but this gave the problem of how to set the preload. Eventually, the parts were assembled by shimming the bearing cap to provide three thousand of preload. The rest of the assembly proved uneventful and it was back to the restorers for refitting.

By September 2006, the bodywork was completed and the car was now a "rolling chassis" with the help of Paul Cooper, a Jaguar classic car specialist.

The rebuilt VSE engine was reinstalled, the adaptor plate on the new gearbox fitted reasonably well to the existing bell housing while having to be fitted from the top. While the E-type was away for bodywork and painting, Dave busied himself with refurbishing the ancillaries. After a year of cleaning, wire brushing and blasting, he was beginning to feel like progress had been made and things were becoming interesting. The mud shields were reworked, blasted and painted before being refitted, while the water transfer pipes were replaced with copper ones.

With hundreds of small parts needing to be re-plated, Dave decided to use to

use a kit from Caswell for the zinc plating of the parts, although he did use a power supply with a higher current capability to increase throughput. With his new plating skills established, Dave then tackled the carburettors, linkages and brackets.

Dave Rawle had been looking for-

ward to the car "taking shape" and had expected this part of the process to be rewarding. However, fitting the chrome trim over a number of days didn't seem to advocate progress and he said: "It has been a challenge". The rewiring proved easier especially with the invaluable sketches and numerous pictures. The dynamo was replaced with an alternator which virtually rendered the ammeter redundant. As a result, Dave replaced it with a period style voltmeter. "123 Ignition" distributor replaced the worn out Lucas unit. This proved cheaper, with fewer moving parts, producing a stronger spark with spark balancing and 16 different advance curves. It was easy to set up and the rebuilt engine fired up at the first turn of the key.

The original Lucas washer pump was replaced by a modern 30 milimetre pump which was held in position by a cable tie both sides of the cap and silicone rubber. While Dave wanted upgrades to provide comfort and reliability, he was not looking to enhance the car's performance. Although he wasn't keen on the idea of slow speed manoeuvring with heavy steering, Dave did want to preserve the "dri-

vability" of the Series 1. Based on a TRW electric pump, he found that Pressure Sensitive Power Steering was the answer. The pump only gives assistance when required by monitoring the effort applied through the steering wheel. But, finding a suitable place to put it was a challenge. Eventually, Dave decided on the area in front of the passenger foot well which required that the brake vacuum tank was moved to the other side of the car under the brake servo. Although the pump was a tight fit, it was a success.

By July 2007, the car was essentially ready for its MOT, which these days, is more rigorous than a basic roadworthy test for vehicles three years old and over. Dave realised that as a car restorer this was a major hurdle and he carefully went through a checklist of brakes, steering,

**RIGHT** At last the
Jaguar is completed

suspension, rubber gaiters, seat belts, lights and wheels. Although, before the all important test, he needed to first fix the boot hinge springs – which he hadn't been looking forward to. However, it wasn't as bad a job as expected. The old springs were "tired" and the new ones were tightly coiled by comparison. The springs were opened by a metal rod so that all five could be interleaved. Next came the number plate chrome beads. These were in poor shape and Dave was disappointed to find that the replacements contained flaws. The right hand bead did not even come close to matching and was only fitted after much bending. Shallower than the originals, the replacements also did not cover the spot welds. With the loose ends tied up, Dave drove 10 miles for the MOT which the car passed.

Even though the car was now roadworthy and legal, there was still work to do, particularly on the brakes and steering. The interior trim was also on the agenda and dynamat was used extensively in order to quell the sound of the tub booming like a drum. Using a trim kit from Aldridge, two types of foam backing were provided, one open cell, the other closed. The open cell required

careful handling as any pressure once the adhesive was applied left a permanent dent. The centre console was to prove difficult. The aluminium and plywood base should, in theory, glue onto the metalwork. Dave found that in practice he had to bolt it on. The car's Heritage Certificate showed the original trim as dark blue piped light blue.

With the braking and steering fixed, Dave turned his attention to fitting the

hood. The fabric itself was the least time consuming part of the job, however, fitting the wooden section to fit the hood frame proved more difficult. This was eventually achieved using a Dremel sanding drum. Dave said: It's vital that the hood frame is adjusted and aligned correctly first". The rear tacking strip was supplied in three sections and needed reworking with the Dremel to ensure a tight fit. The tack-ing strip was wrapped in vinyl which left a flap which could be glued to the inside of the bulkhead.

Once the rear bow is determined, then the webbing can be fitted. Dave discovered that the principle reference point is the rear corner of the windows where the hood must align correctly. For more information on Dave Rawle's restoration please visit: www.davesetype.co.uk

# Other books also available:

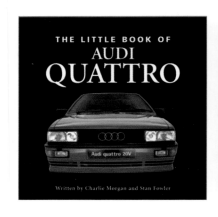

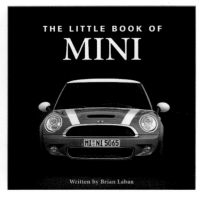